This travel journal belongs to

....

My Today's Adventure

Date...............................

Where I am today................................... The weather today was.........................

My day was: ☐ Awesome ☐ Fun/Cool ☐ OK ☐ Boring

Who was with us: _____

Today we...

My favorite part of today...

_____

_____

_____

_____

_____

Something I learned today...

Draw your today favorite memory...

My Today's Adventure

Date.............................

Where I am today................................. The weather today was.........................

My day was: ☐ Awesome ☐ Fun/Cool ☐ OK ☐ Boring

Who was with us: _____

Today we...

My favorite part of today...

_____

_____

_____

_____

_____

Something I learned today...

Draw your today favorite memory...

My Today's Adventure

Date.............................

Where I am today...................................... The weather today was........................

My day was: ☐ Awesome ☐ Fun/Cool ☐ OK ☐ Boring

Who was with us: _____

Today we...

My favorite part of today...

_____

_____

_____

_____

_____

Something I learned today...

Draw your today favorite memory...

My Today's Adventure

Date..............................

Where I am today... The weather today was........................

My day was: ☐ Awesome ☐ Fun/Cool ☐ OK ☐ Boring

Who was with us: _____

Today we...

My favorite part of today...

_____
_____
_____
_____
_____

Something I learned today...

Draw your today favorite memory...

My Today's Adventure

Date..............................

Where I am today...................................... The weather today was.........................

My day was: ☐ Awesome ☐ Fun/Cool ☐ OK ☐ Boring

Who was with us: _____

Today we...

My favorite part of today...

_____

_____

_____

_____

_____

Something I learned today...

Draw your today favorite memory...

My Today's Adventure

Date.............................

Where I am today...................................... The weather today was.........................

My day was: ☐ Awesome ☐ Fun/Cool ☐ OK ☐ Boring

Who was with us: _____

Today we...

My favorite part of today...

_____

_____

_____

_____

_____

Something I learned today...

Draw your today favorite memory...

My Today's Adventure

Date..............................

Where I am today.. The weather today was.....................

My day was: ☐ Awesome ☐ Fun/Cool ☐ OK ☐ Boring

Who was with us: _____

Today we...

My favorite part of today...

_____

_____

_____

_____

_____

Something I learned today...

Draw your today favorite memory...

My Today's Adventure

Date............................

Where I am today................................. The weather today was......................

My day was: ☐ Awesome ☐ Fun/Cool ☐ OK ☐ Boring

Who was with us: _____

Today we...

My favorite part of today...

_____

_____

_____

_____

_____

Something I learned today...

Draw your today favorite memory...

My Today's Adventure

Date...........................

Where I am today............................... The weather today was.......................

My day was: ☐ Awesome ☐ Fun/Cool ☐ OK ☐ Boring

Who was with us: _____

Today we...

My favorite part of today...

_____

_____

_____

_____

_____

Something I learned today...

Draw your today favorite memory...

My Today's Adventure

Date..........................

Where I am today............................... The weather today was.........................

My day was: ☐ Awesome ☐ Fun/Cool ☐ OK ☐ Boring

Who was with us: _____

Today we...

My favorite part of today...

_____

_____

_____

_____

_____

Something I learned today...

Draw your today favorite memory...

My Today's Adventure

Date........................

Where I am today.................................... The weather today was.......................

My day was: ☐ Awesome ☐ Fun/Cool ☐ OK ☐ Boring

Who was with us: _____

Today we...

My favorite part of today...

_____
_____
_____
_____
_____

Something I learned today...

Draw your today favorite memory...

My Today's Adventure

Date...........................

Where I am today.. The weather today was........................

My day was: ☐ Awesome ☐ Fun/Cool ☐ OK ☐ Boring

Who was with us: _____

Today we...

My favorite part of today...

_____

_____

_____

_____

_____

Something I learned today...

Draw your today favorite memory...

My Today's Adventure

Date............................

Where I am today...................................... The weather today was........................

My day was: ☐ Awesome ☐ Fun/Cool ☐ OK ☐ Boring

Who was with us: _____

Today we...

My favorite part of today...

_____

_____

_____

_____

_____

Something I learned today...

Draw your today favorite memory...

My Today's Adventure

Date................................

Where I am today................................. The weather today was..................

My day was: ☐ Awesome ☐ Fun/Cool ☐ OK ☐ Boring

Who was with us: _____

Today we...

My favorite part of today...

_____

_____

_____

_____

_____

Something I learned today...

Draw your today favorite memory...

My Today's Adventure

Date.............................

Where I am today.................................... The weather today was......................

My day was: ☐ Awesome ☐ Fun/Cool ☐ OK ☐ Boring

Who was with us: _____

Today we...

My favorite part of today...

_____

_____

_____

_____

_____

Something I learned today...

Draw your today favorite memory...

My Today's Adventure

Date...........................

Where I am today............................... The weather today was.......................

My day was: ☐ Awesome ☐ Fun/Cool ☐ OK ☐ Boring

Who was with us: _____

Today we...

My favorite part of today...

_____

_____

_____

_____

_____

Something I learned today...

Draw your today favorite memory...

My Today's Adventure

Date...........................

Where I am today.. The weather today was.........................

My day was: ☐ Awesome ☐ Fun/Cool ☐ OK ☐ Boring

Who was with us: _____

Today we...

My favorite part of today...

_____

_____

_____

_____

_____

Something I learned today...

Draw your today favorite memory...

My Today's Adventure

Date.............................

Where I am today.. The weather today was.........................

My day was: ☐ Awesome ☐ Fun/Cool ☐ OK ☐ Boring

Who was with us: _____

Today we...

My favorite part of today...

_____

_____

_____

_____

_____

Something I learned today...

Draw your today favorite memory...

My Today's Adventure

Date..............................

Where I am today................................... The weather today was.........................

My day was: ☐ Awesome ☐ Fun/Cool ☐ OK ☐ Boring

Who was with us: _____

Today we...

My favorite part of today...

_____

_____

_____

_____

_____

Something I learned today...

Draw your today favorite memory...

My Today's Adventure

Date..............................

Where I am today.................................. The weather today was.........................

My day was: ☐ Awesome ☐ Fun/Cool ☐ OK ☐ Boring

Who was with us: _____

Today we...

My favorite part of today...

_____

_____

_____

_____

_____

Something I learned today...

Draw your today favorite memory...

My Today's Adventure

Date.............................

Where I am today................................... The weather today was.........................

My day was: ☐ Awesome ☐ Fun/Cool ☐ OK ☐ Boring

Who was with us: _____

Today we…

My favorite part of today…

_____

_____

_____

_____

_____

Something I learned today...

Draw your today favorite memory...

My Today's Adventure

Date........................

Where I am today.......................... The weather today was........................

My day was: ☐ Awesome ☐ Fun/Cool ☐ OK ☐ Boring

Who was with us: _____

Today we...

My favorite part of today...

_____

_____

_____

_____

_____

Something I learned today...

Draw your today favorite memory...

My Today's Adventure

Date.............................

Where I am today.................................... The weather today was........................

My day was: ☐ Awesome ☐ Fun/Cool ☐ OK ☐ Boring

Who was with us: _____

Today we...

My favorite part of today...

_____

_____

_____

_____

_____

Something I learned today...

Draw your today favorite memory...

My Today's Adventure

Date...........................

Where I am today... The weather today was.........................

My day was: ☐ Awesome ☐ Fun/Cool ☐ OK ☐ Boring

Who was with us: _____

Today we...

My favorite part of today...

_____

_____

_____

_____

_____

Something I learned today...

Draw your today favorite memory...

My Today's Adventure

Date............................

Where I am today.................................. The weather today was......................

My day was: ☐ Awesome ☐ Fun/Cool ☐ OK ☐ Boring

Who was with us: _____

Today we...

My favorite part of today...

_____

_____

_____

_____

_____

Something I learned today...

Draw your today favorite memory...

My Today's Adventure

Date........................

Where I am today........................ The weather today was........................

My day was: ☐ Awesome ☐ Fun/Cool ☐ OK ☐ Boring

Who was with us: _____

Today we...

My favorite part of today...

_____

_____

_____

_____

_____

Something I learned today...

Draw your today favorite memory...

My Today's Adventure

Date..............................

Where I am today.................................. The weather today was.....................

My day was: ☐ Awesome ☐ Fun/Cool ☐ OK ☐ Boring

Who was with us: _____

Today we...

My favorite part of today...

_____

_____

_____

_____

_____

Something I learned today...

Draw your today favorite memory...

My Today's Adventure

Date........................

Where I am today............................. The weather today was........................

My day was: ☐ Awesome ☐ Fun/Cool ☐ OK ☐ Boring

Who was with us: _____

Today we...

My favorite part of today...

_____
_____
_____
_____
_____

Something I learned today...

Draw your today favorite memory...

My Today's Adventure

Date..........................

Where I am today.................................... The weather today was....................

My day was: ☐ Awesome   ☐ Fun/Cool   ☐ OK   ☐ Boring

Who was with us: _____

Today we...

My favorite part of today...

_____

_____

_____

_____

_____

Something I learned today...

Draw your today favorite memory...

My Today's Adventure

Date...........................

Where I am today.................................... The weather today was.....................

My day was: ☐ Awesome ☐ Fun/Cool ☐ OK ☐ Boring

Who was with us: _____

Today we...

My favorite part of today...

_____

_____

_____

_____

_____

Something I learned today...

Draw your today favorite memory...

My Today's Adventure

Date..........................

Where I am today.. The weather today was......................

My day was: ☐ Awesome   ☐ Fun/Cool   ☐ OK   ☐ Boring

Who was with us: _____

Today we...

My favorite part of today...

_____
_____
_____
_____
_____

Something I learned today...

Draw your today favorite memory...

My Today's Adventure

Date.............................

Where I am today................................... The weather today was........................

My day was: ☐ Awesome ☐ Fun/Cool ☐ OK ☐ Boring

Who was with us: _____

Today we...

My favorite part of today...

_____
_____
_____
_____
_____

Something I learned today...

Draw your today favorite memory...

My Today's Adventure

Date..............................

Where I am today................................... The weather today was.........................

My day was: ☐ Awesome ☐ Fun/Cool ☐ OK ☐ Boring

Who was with us: _____

Today we...

My favorite part of today...

_____

_____

_____

_____

_____

Something I learned today...

Draw your today favorite memory...

My Today's Adventure

Date............................

Where I am today... The weather today was.......................

My day was: ☐ Awesome ☐ Fun/Cool ☐ OK ☐ Boring

Who was with us: _____

Today we...

My favorite part of today...

_____

_____

_____

_____

_____

Something I learned today...

Draw your today favorite memory...

My Today's Adventure

Date............................

Where I am today................................... The weather today was.....................

My day was: ☐ Awesome ☐ Fun/Cool ☐ OK ☐ Boring

Who was with us: _____

Today we...

My favorite part of today...

_____

_____

_____

_____

_____

Something I learned today...

Draw your today favorite memory...

My Today's Adventure

Date............................

Where I am today................................. The weather today was......................

My day was: ☐ Awesome ☐ Fun/Cool ☐ OK ☐ Boring

Who was with us: _____

Today we...

My favorite part of today...

_____

_____

_____

_____

_____

Something I learned today...

Draw your today favorite memory...

My Today's Adventure

Date............................

Where I am today.................................... The weather today was........................

My day was: ☐ Awesome ☐ Fun/Cool ☐ OK ☐ Boring

Who was with us: _____

Today we...

My favorite part of today...

_____

_____

_____

_____

_____

Something I learned today...

Draw your today favorite memory...

My Today's Adventure

Date...........................

Where I am today.................................... The weather today was.....................

My day was: ☐ Awesome ☐ Fun/Cool ☐ OK ☐ Boring

Who was with us: _____

Today we...

My favorite part of today...

_____
_____
_____
_____
_____

Something I learned today...

Draw your today favorite memory...

My Today's Adventure

Date............................

Where I am today................................. The weather today was......................

My day was: ☐ Awesome   ☐ Fun/Cool   ☐ OK   ☐ Boring

Who was with us: _____

Today we…

My favorite part of today…

_____

_____

_____

_____

_____

Something I learned today...

Draw your today favorite memory...

My Today's Adventure

Date............................

Where I am today............................... The weather today was......................

My day was: ☐ Awesome ☐ Fun/Cool ☐ OK ☐ Boring

Who was with us: _____

Today we...

My favorite part of today...

_____

_____

_____

_____

_____

Something I learned today...

Draw your today favorite memory...

My Today's Adventure

Date.............................

Where I am today..................................... The weather today was.....................

My day was: ☐ Awesome ☐ Fun/Cool ☐ OK ☐ Boring

Who was with us: _____

Today we...

My favorite part of today...

_____
_____
_____
_____
_____

Something I learned today...

Draw your today favorite memory...

My Today's Adventure

Date...........................

Where I am today................................... The weather today was.......................

My day was: ☐ Awesome   ☐ Fun/Cool   ☐ OK   ☐ Boring

Who was with us: _____

Today we...

My favorite part of today...

_____

_____

_____

_____

_____

Something I learned today...

Draw your today favorite memory...

My Today's Adventure

Date...............................

Where I am today................................... The weather today was.....................

My day was: ☐ Awesome ☐ Fun/Cool ☐ OK ☐ Boring

Who was with us: _____

Today we...

My favorite part of today...

_____
_____
_____
_____
_____

Something I learned today...

Draw your today favorite memory...

My Today's Adventure

Date............................

Where I am today.. The weather today was........................

My day was: ☐ Awesome ☐ Fun/Cool ☐ OK ☐ Boring

Who was with us: _____

Today we...

My favorite part of today...

_____

_____

_____

_____

_____

Something I learned today...

Draw your today favorite memory...

My Today's Adventure

Date..........................

Where I am today.................................... The weather today was.....................

My day was: ☐ Awesome ☐ Fun/Cool ☐ OK ☐ Boring

Who was with us: _____

Today we...

My favorite part of today...

_____

_____

_____

_____

_____

Something I learned today...

Draw your today favorite memory...

My Today's Adventure

Date...............................

Where I am today.. The weather today was.........................

My day was: ☐ Awesome ☐ Fun/Cool ☐ OK ☐ Boring

Who was with us: _____

Today we...

My favorite part of today...

_____

_____

_____

_____

_____

Something I learned today...

Draw your today favorite memory...

My Today's Adventure

Date...........................

Where I am today.................................... The weather today was......................

My day was: ☐ Awesome ☐ Fun/Cool ☐ OK ☐ Boring

Who was with us: _____

Today we...

My favorite part of today...

_____

_____

_____

_____

_____

Something I learned today...

Draw your today favorite memory...

My Today's Adventure

Date...........................

Where I am today............................... The weather today was.....................

My day was: ☐ Awesome ☐ Fun/Cool ☐ OK ☐ Boring

Who was with us: _____

Today we...

My favorite part of today...

_____

_____

_____

_____

_____

Something I learned today...

Draw your today favorite memory...

My Today's Adventure

Date.............................

Where I am today.................................. The weather today was....................

My day was: ☐ Awesome ☐ Fun/Cool ☐ OK ☐ Boring

Who was with us: _____

Today we...

My favorite part of today...

_____
_____
_____
_____
_____

Something I learned today...

Draw your today favorite memory...

My Today's Adventure

Date.............................

Where I am today................................. The weather today was......................

My day was: ☐ Awesome   ☐ Fun/Cool   ☐ OK   ☐ Boring

Who was with us: _____

Today we...

My favorite part of today...

_____

_____

_____

_____

_____

Printed in Great Britain
by Amazon